Soul Lost, Soul Restored

A Sacred Journey Back to Self

Kathleen McGinley

Editor: Cynthia Krejcsi
www.tailor-made-books.com

cover design: Tailor-Made Books, LLC

cover photograph: Kathleen McGinley

ISBN: 1542505828
ISBN-13: 978-1542505826

Dedication

This book is dedicated to
anyone who ever felt different . . .

Contents

Foreword

These days more and more people are heeding the call to bring their lives into alignment with their soul's purpose. The path of discovery isn't linear and along the way we are faced with any number of challenges, some so dramatic and impactful they cause us to do a complete reevaluation as to how we are living our lives. We're faced with a choice of continuing our lives in a perfunctory manner the way we've always done things or make some tough decisions that alter the trajectory of our life's journey.

These experiences that change our lives and the way we are living often don't make sense to us at the time, but later in looking back at them we may have an "aha!" moment, recognizing the gifts in the experience that were embedded in the passage that moved us through these changes. We may even recognize how God had a hand in those movements, encouraging our emergence into a more spiritually directed and fulfilling life.

A few years ago I had been married to a very successful new age author and for quite a few years everything seemed to be going along very nicely, though in retrospect there were rumblings that I disregarded as my own fears and concerns. Then one day she announced she wanted to separate. I was stunned, angry, hurt, and scared. It felt like I had turned around and been hit by a two by four! There was no convincing her to seek some help and attempt to reconcile.

Thank God for friends. I very soon called on three of my best men friends, and each one of them changed their plans to go for a walk on the beach with me. As we walked along side by side I felt myself shed the illusion of being alone in this travail. I am so grateful even today for these brothers making themselves available to me that day and throughout the coming months as I recovered from the shock. One of my best friends who lived in Florida would call every day for several weeks to check up on me. Even as I recall this I feel an immense gratitude for the love I felt from these men.

Following the abrupt decree from my now ex-wife and the coldness with which it was delivered, for a few days the first words out of my mouth when I woke up were, "Oh, f**k! I'm still alive!" and then I would get up and get on with my day. Now I'm somewhat amused by recalling this period, as I gradually did what I had to do to recover and take good care of myself.

Looking back on this now I am so grateful that this happened. In one of my meditations in which I regularly engaged, the voice of Spirit came to me and explained that this was all very purposeful, in that had we stayed together I would have continued to be overshadowed by her public persona. Further, it was necessary to get me out there on my own, doing the teaching, healing, and writing that I was meant to do. When I heard this it was a revelation – a big "aha!" moment! It provided impetus for me to continue producing several more products that were intended to be of service in other's awakening process.

Herein Kathleen McGinley has shared intimate details of her personal journey, one in which there were a few major "aha!" moments that propelled her into her present mission. She relates her story in a very easy to read and comprehensible manner, as if you were sitting across from her sharing a cup of tea. She encourages the reader in their own journey by providing exercises and guidelines for anyone who has heeded the call to their own awakening process. Though her work is geared primarily to women,

men who are faced with similar concerns can benefit from this book.

One strong thread throughout is how you can face your fears head on and overcome them. Your fears of self-judgment and judgment from others, of failing or even of succeeding, of family's disapproval – all can be confronted and in doing so allow you to emerge further into the human being you were meant to be. You have a purpose here on Earth; and as you continue to align your will with the will of Spirit, you will accomplish that purpose.

As Richard Bach wrote in *The Bridge Across Forever*, "Here is a test to find whether your mission on Earth is finished: If you're alive, it isn't." For Kathleen McGinley, her mission is not finished; and in fact, in one sense it has only begun.

– Dr. Steven Farmer, author of *Animal Spirit Guides*, *Earth Magic*, and *Healing Ancestral Karma*
Website: www.earthmagic.net

Kathleen McGinley

Introduction

About 22 years ago, I had a secret that had me heading for a deep, dark depression. I was desperate, and I needed help. Upon seeing a therapist, I received the diagnosis of *codependency*, a term I had never heard before. After doing some research, I came to the conclusion that she was absolutely right. It was a turning point in my life.

Discovering that I was codependent has not brought me any shame. Rather, it has provided relief as it resolved the confusion I had about my feelings of low self-worth and separateness.

This book is a roadmap of my transformation, describing momentous events that were cathartic and liberating. As a result of my eagerness to do introspection and a determination to change my circumstances, my consciousness began to shift. With time, I no longer saw life as a problem to be solved. Life, even with its challenges, became an adventure to be appreciated.

The stories in this book are not meant to blame or shame anyone from my past. Many specifics of childhood and past relationships are withheld because they are not important. What is most important is to recognize what we have created in our lives and, if we are not happy, to have enough courage to make the necessary changes.

I have written this book for you to discover the three essential components that helped me break my codependent patterns. At the end of their respective chapters, there are exercises that can help you incorporate these components into your life to help you remove the illusion of separation. And, finally, my roadmap takes you to the present day, where I am now sharing my newfound gifts and abilities to help make this world a better place.

My hope is for you to be open to seeing life in a whole new way, filled with miracles and mysticism. It is also my desire that you will see that it is possible to transform a life of unhappiness to a life with meaning and purpose. You are not here to simply spend each day fulfilling your obligations and settling for relationships and jobs that don't make your heart sing. You deserve more. You are here for a reason. Life is to be lived to its fullest. Answer the call.

Chapter 1: My Soul Call

Is this all there is to life? I really never asked myself that question until I was driving to a community center to give private swimming lessons after a full day of teaching high school, taking care of two children, and making dinner for my family. Totally exhausted but proudly stepping into the 'Supermom''role, I felt the need to do whatever it took to provide the best for my family. In my mind, that meant making money so my sons could live in a nice house in the suburbs, wear the trendiest designer clothes, and have all the things that other boys their age had. Heaven forbid that they didn't have friends or get approval from their peers.

The question about life was prompted by the thought I had while driving to my part-time job. My life was mostly about working hard and long hours to make money. Why was so much of my energy focused there? Where did I learn that making money is the most important thing anyone could do?

Looking back, I was doing exactly what my father did. He taught high school all day, coached swimming after school, and then managed a pool as an aquatic director at the community center at night. Except for breakfast and dinner, we hardly ever saw him. I realized that I had become my father!

I can't say that I am not grateful for all that he did. He was a hard-working man who came from a life of poverty and worked his way up to becoming a well-respected, internationally famous, and prosperous man. But this lifestyle wore on him. He worked hard and long so we could have the material possessions that we all aspired to have. But at what cost to the family?

Dad was the breadwinner and wanted the best for us, but he spent many hours away from home. As a little girl, I was desperate for his attention. Even when he was home, my perception was that he was emotionally unavailable and, at times, explosive. I think the stress and long hours of working took its toll on him. Outside of our home, I saw him as the kindest and gentlest human being that ever lived. He was well respected and well known in the community.

My parents showed their love by buying us material things. That was all well and good, but my soul was aching to receive more attention and love from my parents in other ways. I felt very alone. Looking back, I would have preferred hearing "I love you," receiving hugs and kisses, and having heart-to-heart talks during which my opinions would be heard and respected. Instead, my parents' primary way of showing affection was to provide me with "stuff." So my head would justify that they loved me but my heart ached for the real thing.

So when I asked myself the question about the meaning of life that night, I realized that it was really my *soul* calling to me. I knew there had been other *soul calls* in my life, but I had ignored them. I had not understood that they were opportunities for my evolution.

Although this call was a gentle whisper, it got my attention this time. My heart ached when I asked the question about the meaning of life. The Universe knew I was ready to make changes, and my soul was ready to lead the way. It was trying to show me that feeling unhappy and unfulfilled meant that I was not in alignment with my truth. There had to be more to life than I realized.

The Universe led me on a journey where I began to take off my rose-colored glasses. I started to consciously examine my life for the first time. I recognized that although I was married, I was still feeling alone and unhappy. I learned that if I was not satisfied with certain areas of my life, it was up to me to make the changes. I needed to take responsibility for all my pains and all my joys. I needed to wake up.

My question about the meaning of life sparked some events to happen that were beyond my control, including some major shake ups that took me into the darkness of despair. But, in hindsight, these challenges ended up being the best things that could have ever happened to me. It had become time to wake up to who I was, not who everyone else wanted me to be. It was time to be seen and not feel alone anymore.

And so the journey began...

Chapter 2: Loss of Soul

Imagine the feeling that comes with the thought that people don't see you. You think you're invisible. You feel unlovable. You have very few friends. You don't even take time to think about what you want or need because someone tells you how to live and who to be. You feel alone but don't dwell on it because you are focused on responsibilities and obligations. You believe that life is all about taking care of everyone else and living according to other people's expectations.

And then one day a question pops into your mind, *Is this all there is to life?* This is followed by another question, *What can I do about it?* But it stops there because you have no answer.

I believe that when we feel stuck and incapable of making life different, we rarely take the time to consciously look at any options. We have tunnel vision; and if we think of an alternative, we immediately dismiss it because it doesn't seem possible. So we just go through the motions, on auto pilot, and focus on what we need to do to survive.

I didn't even know what I wanted or what was even possible. So how could it be possible that everything I had done up to this point in my life was very successful? I was considered to be an outstanding teacher, both at the school and community center. I had a beautiful home and two beautiful children. People would make comments about my family being perfect. But it wasn't. I was unhappy in my relationship with my husband; but instead of dealing with that, I felt it was more important to make everyone else believe that all was well. After all, one doesn't go telling others about family secrets.

Life, up to this point, lacked deep meaning. I was operating with a loss of soul. It was a feeling of being disconnected, incomplete, and different.[i] On automatic pilot every day, I felt like my purpose was about getting through the day and fulfilling my obligations. I felt like a part of me was missing and my life no longer held the magic that I once believed in. I was always focused on everyone and everything *out there*, making sure I was conforming to societal norms and keeping others happy. But deep down, my soul was craving to be nurtured.

Why do we live in fear of making changes? What makes us live a life that is void of passion? Who wants to live a life that is only filled with obligations and responsibilities? How does this happen?

Change can be frightening. For many people, it is easier to stay in a relationship than to be alone. Too many people are dependent on their spouse/partner and do not feel equipped to live on their own. Finances and children may be some of the reasons one feels the need to stay. Worrying about what everyone else thinks can keep one feeling stuck, too.

Paradoxically, when you feel invisible in a relationship, you can actually feel lonelier than when you are living by yourself with no significant other. Life is all about relationships, so being with someone who cannot fulfill your emotional needs just magnifies the feeling of being alone.

We all have the need to love and be loved. So when the Universe presented an opportunity for a new loving relationship in my life, I thought that would fill the void. Instead, it led me to face the hardest experience of my life. But it also turned out to be the greatest gift.

A New Opportunity

It's funny how we can feel so confident in certain areas of our lives but not in others. I felt I was an excellent high school teacher and had no problem standing in front of the classroom to teach. The feedback I received from both the administration and my students was humbling. But when I found myself in certain social situations with my peers, I felt uncomfortable. I rarely spoke unless I was asked a question. My self-esteem was very low, and I always felt inferior to others and valued their opinions more than my own. I often thought there was something wrong with me. Why did I find it so hard to fit in?

All my life, my energy had been focused on receiving approval and on a strong desire to belong. I was living in fear, always convinced that if I shared my opinion I would be judged and mocked. Feeling like I did not matter was heart wrenching. I would often agree with others even if their opinions were different than my own. As an introvert, I spent a lot of time in solitude; it was safer.

Shortly after I asked the Universe the question about the meaning of life, an opportunity arose that, if taken, would require me to step out of my comfort zone. One day Fern, the President of the Teachers' Union, asked me if I would be interested in serving as a faculty representative for the union. She said she felt I would be a great asset and would have a lot to offer.

Me? What does she see in me that I don't?

Fern assured me that it wouldn't require much of my time and would be relatively easy. I just had to show up at meetings once a month and be available to report to the other teachers on the faculty regarding union issues.

With brief hesitation, I said, "Yes." A wave of fear went through me as I did not know what I was getting myself into, but I felt so much admiration and respect for Fern that I knew I could approach her if I had concerns.

I attended a couple of meetings and found myself, reluctantly, asking a question or offering a suggestion once in a while. Presenting in front of a classroom of high school students was never an issue, but talking in front of my colleagues created anxiety. The fear of judgment from my peers was always a concern. I found my heart racing when I spoke up, but I pushed myself to do this. I was starting to find my voice.

A few months later, Fern asked me to serve on the negotiations committee for the new teachers' contract. I hesitated at first, but the feeling of being appreciated and recognized by an incredible leader who had qualities I aspired to having was enough for me to agree to serve. After the sub-committees were created, the teachers on my sub-committee asked me to serve as the chair.

I began to realize that there were a lot of other teachers out there who had the same fears I did. They, too, had some apprehension about speaking to an audience of their colleagues. After we drafted some ideas regarding a pay scale for extra duties, I was asked to present them to an audience of about 50 other committee members.

I remember taking a few deep breaths. I would consciously take a breath, hold it, and slowly exhale. Without understanding why, I started to relax. It took me out of my head with all of its anxious chatter. I stood up and shared our findings. The room was quiet. People were listening, and I found myself surprised at the respect I was given. My confidence was growing.

Fern had become the pivotal person in my life who opened the door for me to find my voice. She continued to encourage me to step out of my comfort zone by becoming more involved with the union. The more involved I got, the more I grew. It was the beginning of a new chapter in my life, but I was unaware that it was going to be filled with a mix of light and deep darkness.

Filling the Void

"Ask and you shall receive." Well, I had put the question out there and the Universe continued to deliver. The chain of events that happened was far from the ordinary, if not miraculous.

I had been living in denial of my feelings of unhappiness in my relationship with my husband. As far as I knew, marriage was about keeping your husband happy and taking care of the children. Although I did that, my experience felt like I had married a man who was incapable of giving me the love I deeply desired, just like my father.

But as far as I knew, that was what life was all about. My role was to simply fulfill my responsibilities for the household and keep everyone happy. I was living the illusion.

My soul needed to feel loved and wanted to give love. It had become the story of my life. There was no passion in our marriage. Although I was married, I felt alone. My energy in my relationship with my husband was a continuation of my childhood needs. I knew my parents loved me, but I did not recall any verbal or physical expression of love in our family. It felt very conditional, and so I grew up trying to be perfect to be loved.

There were challenges in our marriage; and although they were "red flags," I looked the other way. I minimized things that I should not have because it was more important to me to make the marriage work. When things bothered me, I learned to stuff my feelings. I tried to avoid conflict at all costs.

Shortly after my *soul call*, opportunities presented themselves that got me out of my old routine. As a member of the negotiations team for the teachers' contract, I was offered the chance to meet new people and go to new places. Although feeling anxious at times, I enjoyed the change.

During this time I met a colleague who was kind, affirming, and a great listener. The attention I received from him made my heart sing. It was the first time I was able to discuss personal problems with a man. It was the first time I was able to express my feelings without

9

worrying about being judged. It was the first time I felt heard. It was the first time I felt seen.

A strong emotional attachment began between the two of us. I felt alive and happy when I was around him. In my mind, this blissful feeling was filling the void that lived inside of me and was the remedy for the pain of feeling alone.

Why was I able to hold deep conversations with him but not with my husband? I had a craving to be in his company as much as possible. I no longer felt invisible when I was with him. But on the inside, I was feeling confused and guilty because I was married. I didn't know what to do. Should I live in an unhappy marriage or take action to end it? Out of fear, I felt I was incapable of ending this marriage, so the emotional affair continued.

Reaching Out for Help

The conflict inside my head started to send me into a dark place. I was falling in love with this man. I realized that I needed help. I had not disclosed this situation to anyone. There was no way I could do that. Every day I told myself what a horrible person I was. I knew I had two choices: I either had to muster the courage to seek counseling or I was going to go deeply into depression.

With the feeling of my mind going into a deep darkness, I called the Employee Assistance Program and made an appointment. When I walked into my first session with the therapist, I was asked, "How are you?" I burst into tears, as it had been the first time I felt I could safely release my pent-up emotions. When asked to name the emotions I was feeling about certain things, I had no vocabulary. I was unaware of my feelings! I could name the emotions that other people were experiencing, but I could not name my own.

At the end of the first session, my therapist suggested that I read the book *Codependent No More* by Melody Beattie. Having never heard of the word *codependent*, I was curious and bought the book the next day.

When I got home, I eagerly started to read the book. Although I was not a big reader, I desperately wanted to change my life. As I turned page after page, I felt like I was reading about myself. It was an eye opener. This book changed my life.

Melody Beattie describes a codependent person as someone who gets caught up in other people's problems in order to feel fulfilled. Based on her definition, I allowed another person's behavior to affect me and I obsessed with controlling that person's behavior. [ii]

Control other people's behavior? Me? Ah yes. Sad, but true. When things were not going the way I needed them to go, I would try to change them. In this case, I was trying to change my husband. I was concerned about his drinking and became obsessed with getting him to stop. I had become very codependent in my marriage.

I was so focused on fixing my husband and taking care of everyone else that I had lost my sense of who I was. My self-esteem was damaged, and I was incapable of setting boundaries and expressing my needs. I was externally referenced, basing my worth on everyone else's opinions.

My life was all about getting other people's approval and seeking recognition. I was living from my fear-based ego. But how did I get this way?

In *Codependent No More,* Melody Beattie has the reader explore behaviors that were learned as a child. More often than not, people grow up in some dysfunction related to areas such as their family, peers, religion, and society. Living in survival mode, they develop coping mechanisms and self-protective devices. As we get older, these mechanisms turn into self-destructive behaviors.[iii]

I started to identify the behaviors I'd learned during my upbringing that had affected my capacity to be loved and feel loved in relationships. Based on my interpretation of my childhood experiences, I felt unlovable. I am certain that although my siblings had some of the same experiences, they interpreted them differently. Both my brother and my sister exhibited rebellious behaviors, but I was the compliant middle child.

These are some of the beliefs I had internalized from my parents, peers, church, siblings, and society that had become life-long issues for me:

- Opinions are not to be expressed by females.
- Men are to be put on a pedestal.
- Women are second-class citizens.
- Don't hurt other people's feelings.
- People will not like you if your opinions are different from theirs.
- If you like or love yourself, you are selfish.
- Be good or you will go to hell.

- If your body is not perfect, people will make fun of you.
- You have to be perfect to be loved.
- You are judged by your clothes and material possessions.
- Success is defined by how much money you make.
- Women are not allowed to express their anger.
- Showing sadness or fear is a sign of weakness.

The list goes on and on. What is important to realize is that these are beliefs that are imposed upon us by others. At some point in our lives, we need to do some introspection and determine if these beliefs are really our own! Had we not grown up with our set of parents, belonged to a certain religion, or lived in the United States, how would we feel then? Why are we so afraid to go against what was so ingrained in us?

Taking the first step to healing required me to become aware. Becoming conscious of my thoughts, feelings, and behaviors and understanding the "why" behind them required me to attack my fears of looking within. I had to take responsibility for my life. I had to start living from the inside out. And it was the best thing I ever did.

Activities

My healing began with a willingness to do some introspection. All of my life, I had been living from the outside in, but now it was time to live from the inside out. This required me to review my past and try to understand my thoughts, feelings, and behaviors.

The following activities include some of the questions I asked myself. Take some time to ask yourself these questions and get to know yourself. It will be the beginning of the journey to discover the beautiful soul that you are.

1.   Where was most of your energy focused as a child? What were your unmet needs? How did that translate into your adult world?

2.   What are some of your learned beliefs from parents, siblings, teachers, peers, religion, and society that have become life-long issues for you?

3. Are you doing what you love? Are there any "shoulds" that are directing your life, or are you designing it the way you want to? What keeps you from having the life you want?

4. For the next 24 hours, imagine that you were just born. You have no fears, no learned beliefs, no complaints, and no opinions. You see everything as a miracle. Describe your experience.

Chapter 3: The First Essential Component for Healing— Connecting with the Universe

Upon accepting that I was codependent, I became free from all those years of blaming and disliking myself for being different and from feeling unlikable and unlovable. I was now beginning to understand my thoughts, feelings, and actions. Much of the feedback and messages that I had internalized from my parents, teachers, relatives, peers, church, and society had created my feelings of shame and low self-worth. As I looked back over my life, I determined that they were other people's beliefs that were imposed on me. It was time to take my life back!

I was committed to change, not realizing that there were three essential components for me to do so. As I went through my recovery, I began to discover the components that led to my healing. Some of them included strategies that were very practical, while others were quite mystical.

The recovery process for me was very liberating and at times fun! Engaging in self-discovery was intriguing. Shedding some of my old belief systems helped me attain personal freedom and be at peace with who I am.

So when I asked myself what I needed to do to heal, the Universe was ready to lead the way. When I returned to my next session with my therapist, she suggested that I attend Codependents Anonymous (CoDA), a 12-step program for codependency. All I knew was that it was a meeting with others who were like me who desired healthy and loving relationships.[iv] I had no idea what I was getting into. She made me promise that I would attend at least five sessions. This created a lot of anxiety. But I promised her that I would attend, and I was pretty good at keeping promises.

A few days later, I reluctantly walked into my first meeting, which was held at a church. There were at least 20 other men and women in the room, sitting on chairs in a circle. The group leader passed out handouts, and we were given the guidelines and format of the meeting. I glanced at the paper that listed the 12 steps and saw the word *spiritual.* I read, "Having had a *spiritual* awakening as a result of these steps..." [v]

Oh no! Was this some religious group? There was no way I wanted anything to do with religion. Was this some kind of cult? I was ready to walk out the door.

Religion? Hell, NO!

I sat there in a state of anxiety and wanted to leave so badly. Of course, I did not. I had a therapy session coming up and I had promised that I would go to this meeting. I was always a rule follower.

The leader started to read the handouts and said something about a *Higher Power*.[vi] I assumed this meant *God.* Immediately, I was taken back to my religious days in the Catholic Church. All I could think of was how religion made me feel like a bad person and *God* was going to send me to hell if I wasn't perfect. The fear permeated every cell of my body, thinking that I was being judged in every moment.

However, I stayed and began to listen to people's stories. I soon realized that I was not alone. Their stories sounded like mine. There were people like me! This was not therapy because there was no advice giving or cross talk. We were simply there to go over the 12 steps and apply them to our lives. We focused on *our own* feelings for a change. So I decided to go back for more sessions, as I had promised my therapist.

After a couple of sessions, I began to understand that a *Higher Power* wasn't about a man with supernatural powers sitting on a cloud, punishing me if I made bad choices. I learned that I had the freedom to choose to create a new concept of *God*, based on *my* beliefs. This *Higher Power* would simply be defined as something loving and greater than me.[vii] From what I heard others saying, their concept of *God* had become a loving presence that not only was the creator of the Universe but was *in* everything, including me.

All this time I had been living in fear. This alternative way of thinking made me realize that if *God* lived inside of me I, too, was a co-creator of my life. There was no separation and, therefore, no judgment coming from out there. I needed to take responsibility for all my pain and all my pleasures. I decided to pay attention and see if I could create a relationship with my *Higher Power* and determine if this loving *God* really existed. I had nothing to lose, so I told myself I would *fake it until I made it*. And the miracles started to happen.

Coincidence?

One dark and dreary day, I grabbed one of my self-help
books on codependency. (To this day I can't remember
which book it was.) I bundled up in some blankets, sat on
my bed with my back propped up against my headboard,
and started to read about a story of a woman named
Kathy. This woman always needed to have her house look
perfect. Everyone who came to visit would always remark
about how clean and organized she kept her house. Little
did they know that if you were to open any of her closets,
you would see they were filled to the brim with "stuff."
Her house was pretty much a metaphor of her mind, still
hiding things about herself to avoid being judged as
imperfect. It sounded like the story was about me!

As I continued to read, there was a sentence that read
something like this: "And then one day, the sun came into
her house and shone brightly, and the woman started to
wake up..." At the very moment I was reading this
passage, the sun came out; a beam of light came through
the window and shone right on that paragraph. I got the
chills. What just happened? Was that a coincidence? Was
that my *Higher Power*?

I took it as a possible sign and continued to become
conscious of other synchronicities. I knew I had nothing
to lose. I made a decision to continue to believe and tap
into this *Higher Power*, asking for guidance. As I became
more aware, there were other things that started to happen
that were totally out of my control but led me where I
needed to go.

Sacred Path Cards

As I was trying to get clear about my concept of my *Higher Power*, I decided to go to a book store and research spirituality. I stumbled upon a book and deck of cards called *The Sacred Path Cards* by Jamie Sams. The 44 beautifully illustrated cards came with a book about Native American spirituality with lessons of self-discovery. Paying attention to my thoughts, I heard an old voice saying, "Cards are the work of the devil." I knew this belief was from the Catholic Church and not my own. I had never used cards before, but I was open to the experience. Totally into learning more about myself, I bought them.

When I got home, I immediately read the instructions and found that I simply had to be clear with my questions. I lit a candle and shuffled the cards, hoping to receive some guidance about my challenging situations.

Faced with these three major life-changing decisions, I asked my *Higher Power*, whom I often refer to as *Spirit*, to give me direction regarding my relationship, my part-time job, and my place of employment. After asking the first question about my affair, I pulled the "Shaman's Death" card. The illustration on the card was quite scary. I reluctantly opened the book to read about the interpretation. The message of the card was that I needed to end the relationship. Doing so would lead to the "death" of my old identity. viii

I then asked the second question about my part-time job as secretary of the teacher's union. Once again, I pulled

"Shaman's Death." Two minutes later, I asked the third question about transferring out of the high school where I presently taught. And still again, I pulled "Shaman's Death."

What are the chances that I would pull the same card three times in a row within five minutes? I sat there wonderstruck. The cards confirmed my thoughts that I needed to quit my part-time job, teach at a different school, and end the affair. It was time for me to consciously remove parts of my shadow and re-invent myself. From that day forward, I realized that these cards spoke to my soul; and I have continued to use them as a guidance system ever since.

Nature's Guidance System

As I read more and more about Native American spirituality, I discovered that I had found my truth. The teachings were in alignment with my own thoughts about the world around us. Like the Native Americans, I believed that everything in nature had a Spirit. As a young child, I played daily in the woods behind my home. The forest was my sanctuary. I loved climbing the trees, turning over the rocks, and feeding the squirrels. I felt alive when I was communing with nature.

I felt a strong pull to connect with a Native American and learn more about Native American mystical ways. I felt that both the visible as well as the unseen world had so much to tell us. My need to explore the intangible was intense.

While I was still struggling to end my relationship with my lover, I stumbled upon an article in the newspaper about a local shaman named Shadow Wolf. I felt compelled to meet her. I found her phone number and left a voice message but did not get a call back. A couple of weeks later, I went to a spiritual expo at the Allentown Fairgrounds and noticed that she had a booth and was giving readings. I signed up reluctantly, as I never had a psychic reading from someone else before.

Shadow Wolf called in her Spirit Guides and proceeded to intuitively tell me about my life. She somehow knew about the relationship with my lover and was concerned about my well-being. She offered great guidance and insight. Her psychic abilities blew me away, and I felt drawn to learning as much as I could from her.

At the end of the session, I told her I had left a message on her phone. She explained that her two-year-old had erased all the voice messages that day, which was why she was unable to call me back. It was synchronistic that we found each other. From that day forward, she became a mentor as well as a good friend.

Shadow Wolf felt that I would resonate with Ted Andrews' book *Animal-Speak*. According to Andrews, at one time humanity recognized that we are part of nature and nature is part of us. He felt that we are capable of communicating with everything in nature, whether it is an animal, insect, bird, or reptile. These are our allies in nature, giving us messages and guidance through symbolism when we honor their power. We just need to ask and then pay attention because nature will teach those who are open to learning from her.[ix]

Shadow Wolf was right. This book became my bible. My ability to read signs in nature became greater. Shadow Wolf explained to me that I could create my own communication system with the animals, birds, insects, and reptiles. She gave me the example of how she communicated with hawk. If he were to fly clockwise, she knew her prayers would be answered.

I began to create my communication system and watch the behaviors of the various creatures. I paid attention to what creatures were showing up unusually or repetitively. I studied their attributes. By doing so, I began to intuitively know what many of them were trying to tell me.

One day I was driving to a coffee shop in my new Jeep Cherokee. On the way, I noticed a hawk on top of a telephone pole. He turned his head to the right and then to the left. I didn't think anything of it at the time. After I finished my coffee at the shop, I got into my car and drove out of the lot to turn left at the traffic light.

As I approached the green light at the intersection, I noticed a car in the lane on my right that proceeded to turn onto the highway. Upon moving into the road to make my left turn, I saw a truck heading right at me. He was on my left, not braking, and traveling at a high rate of speed. There was no way that I was *not* going to get hit. In that moment, I knew I was either going to die or get seriously injured. I accelerated for a split second, just enough so that his truck hit my car in the area of my back seat. I spun around twice and got trapped in the car, but I was fortunate to escape without serious injury.

Was I getting a message from hawk to warn me? It is my belief that the hawk was trying to get my attention to tell me to look both ways.

There is no separation between us and the world around us. If we commune with nature, I believe we can get all the messages and guidance we need. I feel that the world is our mirror and what we perceive is happening around us is also a reflection of what is happening inside of us.

Mystical Dreams

One thing I started to recognize early on was that my dreams had become very clear and vivid. I knew there had to be deeper meanings, so I made it a point to remember them and write them down as soon as I woke up.

At a spiritual expo I found a dream interpretation book called *DreamSpeak*, authored by Helen and Lou White Bear, which really resonated with me. The book included a small dictionary that interpreted the meaning of many symbols found in dreams, such as numbers, colors, the alphabet, buildings, cars, animals, and many other things. Using this guide to interpret my dreams helped me understand the state of my mind. It also gave me guidance on how to proceed with my challenges. I felt that my Spirit Guides knew how I was going to interpret my dreams, so they gave me exactly the images I needed to see.

What I liked about *DreamSpeak* is that it had some unusual ways of interpretation. One example of this was that I was to pay attention to teachers who showed up in my dreams. I would take their names apart and the syllables would give me a message.[x] For example, Bill was a forewarning that I was going to B-ill or "be ill." It was usually correct.

I also received a lot of other messages from the syllables of teachers' last names. For example, a teacher in my department would appear periodically in my dreams. I interpreted her last name, Cruttenden, as C-rut-enden, or "See rut ending." It would tell me that the stagnation period was over. I loved getting that message when my life was at a standstill.

As I was going through this trying time in my life, I occasionally had "death" dreams. I literally would die in my dream. Often I was approached by a man with a rifle. He would shoot me in the neck, and I would feel myself die.

Rather than getting scared and upset by these dreams, I interpreted them to be symbolic of the death of an old identity. Part of my shadow needed to be released so I could become more of my authentic self. Now I know what it feels like to die; it doesn't scare me anymore.

Shifting to an inward focus made me realize that I had some gifts of prophesy. I would occasionally have a dream that was precognitive. One stood out that still gives me chills to this day. It happened during my transitional period in the mid-90's when I was to chaperone a field trip with my students to the Southwest. I had a nightmare the night before I was to pay for my airfare.

In my dream, I witnessed a skyscraper burning. People were jumping out of the building. Then it happened again. After that, I saw an American Airlines jet taking off of a runway. I woke up crying and sweating. I never had dreams with that intensity. I didn't know what to make of it. All I thought was that it was a warning that I should not pay for my airfare but cancel my trip instead.

The next morning, I backed out as a chaperone as the dream felt too real. The trip went on without me and all was well. Little did I know that my dream was the same scene that would occur a few years later on 9/11.

Many people believe that dreams are not important and should be ignored. Based on my experience, I know they have meaning and that our Guides use them to give us the clarity we need to make decisions.

Feel and Deal

As I continued to engage in self-discovery, I started to become an observer of my life. Every day I was becoming more aware of my thoughts and feelings. I was starting to understand who I was and taking responsibility for creating the unfulfilling life that I had.

Identifying my emotions was not easy. I had been so focused on everyone else and their feelings that I did not have a handle on what I was feeling. Being externally focused enabled me to shut down the unpleasant feelings that were brewing inside. Subconsciously, I had been holding in years of sadness and anger. I *was* my emotion instead of just *feeling* my emotion. I knew that I had to stay busy and look outside of myself to avoid these feelings.

But it was time to learn about me. As I continued to read self-help books, I got a better understanding of who I was. I also began paying attention to what my beliefs were, as well as my interests. It amazed me how much people pleasing I did. I would often do things or say things just to get other people's approval. In my mind, it was more important for me to agree with them because I was so afraid to be judged if I were *different*.

This was all new territory for me. I was learning that in order to heal, I must feel. But feeling emotions was scary. Growing up, I felt that my feelings and opinions would be judged harshly if they were not in agreement with my parents' opinions. So I learned to shut them down.

"Feel and deal" became my mantra. Because I had shut down emotions for most of my life, I had to now ask my *Higher Power* to help me feel. And boy, did I ever.

Gasping for Air

After a few months in counseling and attending CoDA, I came out of denial about a lot of things in my marriage. I was finally not looking the other way. There were events that were occurring with my husband and his drinking that fueled my anger. At times I felt so angry I was unable to speak. I was afraid of his temper. And when I felt the dysfunction was affecting our children, I had enough courage and a support system to express my feelings and ask for a separation. On Independence Day, my husband moved out.

I was getting stronger every day but still lived in a lot of fear. How will I be able to live on my own? What are others going to think? How angry will my husband get if I file for divorce? Why am I so afraid of him? Instead of grieving our relationship, I looked outside of myself to comfort my fears.

The relationship with the man outside of my marriage went to a new level of intimacy. It felt like an addiction. The problem was that he was married. As much as I felt a love like I never felt before, I knew it was wrong and tried to sever it a few times, only to return to this unhealthy obsession.

Meanwhile, my connection with my *Higher Power* was growing stronger. Every day I would ask the Universe for help, and within 24 hours I would notice coincidences. Synchronicities occurred that supported me in moving forward and giving me the answers that I was seeking. I was now coming to know that there really was something greater than myself.

Slowly, I was able to take off my rose-colored glasses about my lover. Although he was admired in the community for his leadership, I perceived his actions to be very controlling. I found him driving by my house at 11 p.m. one night when I had a friend over. Seeing her Datsun 280Z outside my house prompted him to call me to make sure I was not cheating on him. My mind instantly went to the thought that it was okay for him to have a wife...but I couldn't date?

Although my inner voice was telling me to end this relationship, I still found it hard to break things off. I had tried several times, only to go back later. But the Universe knew I needed to get stronger before giving me a "kick in the butt."

One afternoon, I was at a function with my son and in walked my lover with his wife and kids. They looked like the typical All-American family, happy and loving. My heart sank. I had been asking for clarity...but this was a reality that was hard to bear. It was the straw that broke the camel's back.

I went home, paced back and forth in my bedroom, and started to talk aloud. The anger that was inside of me started to surface. I made a commitment to myself that I would end this relationship and never be controlled by another man again. Finally, the rage erupted from the pit of my stomach and my body shook like it was seizing. It felt as if the release valve had been opened. When there was no more steam, only grief remained.

The sobbing started, but I knew that it was okay to feel. I knew that I was going to be protected by my *Higher Power*. So I continued to ask my *Higher Power* to help me "feel and deal." Later, I made a phone call to my lover and ended the relationship. The pain had exceeded the love. I was committed to it being over this time.

Every day the sobbing continued as the grief got stronger. I found myself running to the bathroom at work to avoid being seen as this roller coaster of emotions would come out of nowhere. There was no one I could talk to about this relationship because I felt guilty and knew it was wrong. The pain in my heart grew stronger every day.

On the ninth day of grieving, the pain became so intense that I thought I was going to die. Little did I know that I was experiencing "broken heart syndrome," a pathological disorder that mimics a heart attack and can be fatal.[xi]

By the time I got home from work, I felt as if I were suffocating. My heart had become enlarged, and I was being deprived of oxygen. The pain in my chest hurt so badly it felt like I was having a heart attack. I slowly crawled up the steps to my bedroom on the second floor, gasping for air. I feared that I was going to die and my kids would come home to find their mother lying dead on the bedroom carpet.

I crawled on my hands and knees over to my bedroom window, barely able to pull myself up to the window sill, looked up to the bright blue sky and the light of the sun, and somehow was able to say these words aloud,

> "Please take this pain away and replace it with love for you and love for myself."

In that very moment, the pain stopped. What just happened? It was as if a switch had been turned off. A feeling of calm overcame me, as if I was part of everything and everything was part of me. I sat there in a state of wonderment.

I had just conquered the hardest thing I ever had to do in my life. My surrendering to the Universe miraculously made the intense pain disappear. There was not one ounce of chest pain left. This experience not only validated my *belief* in my *Higher Power*, but now I had come to *know* it.

I sat there and realized that I had just experienced a miracle. I was returning to myself.

Activities

Shifting from being externally referenced to becoming an observer of my own life required me to face my fears of introspection. I was initially afraid to look within because of the perceived intense pain that might occur because I did not like myself. However, by connecting with something greater than myself, I felt protected.

Below are some of the activities that helped me connect with my *Higher Power*. The more you become conscious of the synchronicities and messages that you are being sent, the more trust you will have that there is something greater.

1. Describe your concept of a *Higher Power*. Create a new concept if you see your *Higher Power* as fearful, judging, or separate from you.

2. To deepen your connection with your *Higher Power*, try this: Go outside, look up into the sky, and ask your *Higher Power* to help you establish a deep connection. With heartfelt emotion, recite this prayer: "In trust and gratitude, I ask for your love and protection. Please fill my heart with love for you and help me love myself more and more each day. I surrender my will to you. Thank you for your guidance." Take a moment to feel your heart space open and visualize it filling with light and love. Repeat this as often as you'd like. Write about your experience.

3. When a situation arises and you need guidance, repeat this prayer and ask your *Higher Power* to give you signs and messages. Become conscious of the synchronicities that take place in the next 24 to 48 hours. Journal any synchronicities that occur as a reminder when you slip into fear and lack of trust.

4. Pay attention to which animals, insects, birds, or reptiles are showing up in your life unusually or repetitively. Watch their behaviors and listen to your mind interpret the spiritual message. Think of their attributes to help with the interpretation. For example, if you see a woodpecker pecking like crazy, you might think of the word *determination.* His message is telling you to keep at it! What messages do the creatures have for you?

5. Before you go to sleep, ask you Spirit Guides to help you remember your dreams. Keep a journal at your bedside and write them down as soon as you awaken. Try to interpret them with your own system or a dream book that resonates with you.

Chapter 4: The Second Essential Component for Healing— Connecting with Self

I had totally disconnected from my lover. The grieving was over. My marriage was over. It might appear that I was alone physically...but I was not lonely. Something happened in that moment of surrender that made me feel that I was one with the Universe. There was no separation. I couldn't explain it, but it was as if I had become a part of everything. I felt as though the world was my mirror and the answers were all around me.

But my work was not over. It was really just beginning. It was up to me to continue to engage in self- discovery and determine what I needed to do to advance my healing and know myself completely.

So the first question I asked myself was *Why?* Why did I attract the unhealthy relationships into my life? It didn't take long for me to see that although these types of relationships were not what I wanted, they were what I was used to. I was actually comfortable with the drama. That's what I knew. But in my surrender, I was determined to let go of the drama in my life. I had had ENOUGH!

This whole experience was a realization that I needed to start loving myself more and re-wire my brain. I had so many negative thoughts about myself, almost to the point of self-hate. As a child, I was constantly focused on what was wrong with me instead of my good qualities. This included body image. My parents were very health conscious and image was important. My mother, who aspired to be an actress, would often apologize for giving me the body that I had. She and I were built the same, sporting small breasts and large hips. No matter how much weight I would lose, my body proportions would remain the same. This led me to having a distorted body image as a young adult. When I look back at the years I thought I was fat, I was actually very thin. It saddens me to think that I had such negative self-talk, when in fact there was no reason to believe that.

I also felt guilty about the affair and would often say hateful things to myself. There were times I would actually hear myself condemning me to hell. There were still beliefs from the Catholic religion that had me living in fear. Beating myself up most of the time was normal, and I needed to learn how to stop it.

Fortunately, between CoDA and self-help books, I found techniques to help me re-wire my brain. It was time to focus within. I began to recognize the messages that I would say to myself that were harmful. My thoughts had become my reality. It was necessary for me to start becoming very conscious of what I would say to myself.

One of the most valuable tools that I learned was reciting affirmations. *Affirmations* are statements affirming what you want in life. They are new beliefs that you want to create about yourself.[xii]

I would become conscious of my negative thought, reword it into a positive thought, and state it in the present tense.

If the affirmation felt too difficult to say because it felt like I would be lying to myself, I would add the words *willing to*. So my mental thoughts were slowly and consciously being re-wired, from *I am unlovable* to *Every day I choose to love myself more*. Eventually my words became *I love myself!* And I started to believe it!

What was even more powerful was when I repeated my affirmations while looking into my eyes in the mirror. It was as if I was looking into my soul. Loving myself was difficult at first; but when I thought of myself as a young child, I would imagine I was talking to her. So I would change the affirmations and speak in second and third person point of view as well. When I said, *You are lovable* or *Kathy is lovable,* it would shift the origin of the thought.

When one does not love herself unconditionally, it affects all other relationships. Why would anyone love you if you don't love yourself? People who are attracted to those who feel unlovable feel unlovable themselves, but they also know they can easily control and manipulate others who do not love themselves. Often when we don't love ourselves we are unable to say "no" and will do almost anything to feel loved by another.

My Epiphany

Although I had been reciting my affirmations and feeling better about myself, there was still something missing. I needed to feel it on a deeper level. And then one day, I had an epiphany. I read a quote from Marianne Williamson's book *Return to Love*. It read:

"Our deepest fear is not that we are inadequate. Our deepest fear is that we are powerful beyond measure. It is our light, not our darkness that most frightens us. We ask ourselves, 'Who am I to be brilliant, gorgeous, talented, fabulous?' Actually, who are you not to be? You are a child of God. Your playing small does not serve the world. There is nothing enlightened about shrinking so that other people won't feel insecure around you. We are all meant to shine, as children do. We were born to make manifest the glory of God that is within us. It's not just in some of us; it's in everyone. And as we let our own light shine, we unconsciously give other people permission to do the same. As we are liberated from our own fear, our presence automatically liberates others."

I'm a "child of God"? Having experienced my miracle with a *knowing* that there is a *Higher Power (God)* and that I have been given the opportunity to experience life on this earthly plane, *how dare I not love myself!* I am not here to try to be like everyone else or get them to like me. I am here on earth to discover and claim my uniqueness. I am a spiritual being, temporarily living in this physical body, with my mission to know myself, discover my gifts, and help make this world a better place.

As my love for myself continued to grow, I noticed that my relationships with others changed as well. People started to treat me with more respect. Now I understood the saying, "People will treat you the way you treat yourself." As this self-love continued to grow, I realized how it was interrelated with all the other aspects of wellness. The more I loved myself, the more I was willing to nurture myself and put myself before others. Slowly, I was able to reverse my belief that it would be selfish to take care of myself first. I learned that I was better able to take care of others after I took care of my own needs. Although I now put myself before others, my *Higher Power* was still at the top of my list.

Setting Intentions

More and more, I began to see how my thoughts were creating my reality. As I became more aware of what I was thinking, I was able to turn any pessimistic or negative thought into something positive. I would also consciously determine *why* I was thinking, feeling, or considering an action. If I felt my contemplated action was coming from fear or ego, I would choose a different behavior. It had become so important for me to be in integrity with my truth and remain as authentic as possible.

I started to create rituals that would help me manifest what I not only wanted in life but what I deserved. One morning, I took a thin lock of my short hair and braided it with intentions. As I wove each strand, I stated how I wanted my day to unfold as well as how I wanted to show up for that day. I started with the words *I am...* and kept it positive and affirming. It set the stage for each day; and magically, my intentions would be met.

In the Moment

I realized that my thoughts were often concerns about the past or the future that kept me from experiencing the present moment. If the thoughts were disconcerting, it caused stress. However, if I were to remain present, all was well.

How many of us are often not in the here and now? How do we stay there and keep our minds from repeating the same thoughts over and over?

I began using meditation as one of my tools that helped me stay in the present. In *Finding Your Sacred Self*, Susan Gregg defines *meditation* as thinking in a contemplative manner. She writes that it is an essential skill for those who want to know themselves.[xiii]

I practiced meditation by closing my eyes and focusing on my inhalation and exhalation for a few minutes daily. When I focused on my breath, I was unable to think of anything else. If my mind did start to wander, I went back to my breath. This began to train my brain to be focused on what was taking place all around me. I became better able to see all the miracles that were happening around me because I was no longer lost in thought.

Often we are so busy doing things that we don't give ourselves time to just "be." Sometimes staying busy is a way to avoid feeling our emotions. When we slow down, it is possible that feelings will begin to surface. When this happens, it is a great opportunity to feel the emotions and let them move through us. Emotions are our allies and we do not need to fear them. We do not have to let them control us. Learning to be in the moment will help us respond, rather than react, to life's challenges.

Visualizations

Visualizations have become an important tool for manifesting what I want and how I want to show up. In their book *Empowerment,* Gershon and Straub define *visualization* as a mental image or picture of what you want to create in your life. Using visualization together with an affirmation creates the best results.[xiv] I learned by accident that if you can't visualize what you want, it probably won't happen.

Years ago, when my husband and I were trying to start a family, I was unable to become pregnant. We tried unsuccessfully for a year and a half, with both of us having tests run by doctors. The tests always came back normal. Finally, my gynecologist suggested that I make an appointment with the Hershey Medical Center because it had more sophisticated technology. Meanwhile, he gave me fertility pills to start taking after I got my next period.

I immediately called the Hershey Medical Center. However, they couldn't see me for two months. I lay down on my bed and cried, but then I closed my eyes and tried to see myself as pregnant. I couldn't! No matter how hard I tried, the image of me with a big belly was not there.

For the next three days, I tried to see myself as pregnant. Finally, on the third day, I could see the big belly! The emotions that came with the image were that of pure joy! All I could do now was look forward to getting my period in a couple of weeks so I could start taking the fertility pills.

My period never came! I had become pregnant. How did this happen? Had I erased a mental block by visualizing? This experience made me realize how important it is to visualize what it is that we want to manifest.

Since then, I have created visualizations with images of how I have wanted to show up in life. Examples included seeing myself calmly relating to others who were intimidating me as well as confidently presenting in front of large audiences. Each image evoked a positive feeling that I allowed to move through every cell of my body. And, gratefully, these visualizations helped me energetically shift from codependency to a new way of being.

Trusting the Universe

When I need assistance from the Universe, I give thanks in advance to show the trust I have in my *Higher Power*. My relationship with my *Higher Power* is 24/7 and the connection is strong. When I ask *Spirit*, whom I have come to recognize as the energy of *God* and part of me, for help in the manifestation of my dreams or assistance in dealing with a difficult situation, I know things will turn out exactly as they are supposed to.

Whenever I feel that things are not going my way, I take a moment to reflect on my thoughts about what I want and what I deserve. I examine my limiting belief systems to see if they are creating a block. As a co-creator of the Universe, I know that my thoughts and words are creating my reality. Therefore, I take the time to ask myself questions such as "Why am I doing this?" or "Do I feel I deserve this?" or "What am I really asking for?" If necessary, I alter my limiting beliefs to become more aligned with my truth.

If my belief systems are positive and strong, I look at the amount of my energy that is trying to control the outcome. If my energy is getting in the way of the energy of the Universe, I have to surrender. God works in mysterious ways, and I have to trust that I will be led to wherever I need to go or whatever I need to do. If the outcome is different than what I had hoped for, often in hindsight I understand why. I have found that there's a reason for everything.

Activities

Learning to live from the inside out has created personal freedom for me. It required me to be conscious of what I say to myself, knowing that I will become who I think I am. I knew that if I wanted to show up differently, I needed to reprogram my brain.

These are some of the activities that helped me connect with my truth. Remember that you have years of programming. It takes awhile to rewire. Don't give up. You are worth it!

1. Pay attention to your self-talk. Write down any negative things you say to yourself regarding your self-esteem and self-worth. Change each statement to an affirmation. Make sure it is positive and in the present tense. (Don't use any negative words.)

    Look into the mirror and recite the affirmations daily, as often as possible. Place Post-it® Notes with the affirmations around the house to remind you.

2. Identify your uncomfortable or unhealthy behaviors when you relate to others. Lie down and visualize how you would like to respond differently in these situations. Feel the emotion that you would like to feel with your desired outcome. Visualize this as often as you can. Write about your experience.

3. Create a ritual for setting intentions. (I created a ritual with braiding my hair.) Think of how you want to show up as well as what you want to manifest. Start with *I am grateful that I am...* or *I have....* Change your intentions based on what you

need for that day. Write down any manifestation that occurs to remind you that the Universe is working with you.

4. Practice your ritual for meditation. What time of day is best for you? Where will you do this? Describe your experience.

Chapter 5: The Third Essential Component for Healing— Connecting with Others

Life is about relationships. When we look at our existence here on earth, we have to realize that we are in relationship with everything. We develop relationships with people, animals, plants, computers, food, and anything else we come in contact with. The more satisfying relationships we have, the more we will enjoy life. Therefore, developing healthy interpersonal skills that are based on love, not fear, can be the most important thing we do.

Soul Sharing

I continued to attend the CoDA meetings and learned how to focus on my feelings. Only one person in the group was allowed to speak at a time while sharing his/her story with his/her feelings. There was no blaming or shaming other people when we spoke. We were also instructed that there was to be no advice giving or interrupting. We were there simply to listen. We were learning how to move out of the victim role and take total responsibility for our lives.

Initially, I very rarely shared. I was still in a space of being concerned about what other people would think of me. I found it very interesting that I had no fear when it came to teaching students, but when it came to my peers and authority figures, I shut down.

Slowly, I started to face my fears and share my stories periodically. It amazed me that people sat and listened. I was finally learning how to become internally referenced as I became more conscious of my thoughts and feelings. Being vulnerable and sharing my soul with others was one of the most courageous things I ever did.

When it came to other social situations, one of the hardest things for me to do was assert myself. If somebody did something that offended or hurt me, I would often become passive and not say anything. Any kind of confrontation scared the living daylights out of me. But with new tools such as "I messages," I faced my fears and started to speak up. An "I message" begins with the word *I* and is an assertion about the feelings, beliefs, or values of the person who is speaking.

Simply stating "I feel...when...," followed by citing the inappropriate behavior of the other person, allowed me to safely assert myself. It became a way of taking responsibility for my feelings as opposed to blaming or shaming the other person.

Understanding that my opinions and feelings are never wrong made it easier to express them. It was awkward at first, but with time it became automatic. It felt like my voice was getting stronger. It was very empowering. I was learning to take care of myself instead of worrying that I might hurt other people's feelings. It became a time to protect myself instead of everyone else.

New Adventures

Now that I had a trusting relationship with the Universe, I felt protected and guided at all times. I was not in any relationship with a man, nor was I dating, so I had plenty of freedom to do what I wanted. I continued to face my fears over the next year by making an effort to try new things.

There were times when I would go out to dinner or to the movies on my own. I also took some road trips, some solo and some with my two boys. One trip with my boys was very spontaneous. I said, "Pack your bags. Let's go to the shore tomorrow!" It was one of the best vacations I ever had...and very empowering.

Interestingly enough, one year after my divorce, the Universe presented me with another opportunity that was hugely transformational. As a public school teacher, I was required to take more continuing education credits. As I searched the courses available, I found one in Harrisburg, Pennsylvania, that sounded interesting because it had the word *adventure* in the class description. I really didn't want to drive a total of three hours to and from class every week, but I kept feeling pulled to sign up for this course. Little did I know that I was about to embark on something that was life changing!

The class was entitled "Adventure Programming," and the only thing I knew was that it was about creating adventurous programs for the students in the classroom. It sounded perfect for teaching Physical Education at the high school level.

The facilitators of this course were quite knowledgeable as they guided us with fun, experiential activities in the classroom. What I came to understand was that these programs were to help people become conscious of their thoughts, feelings, and behaviors as they engaged in these group problem-solving activities. It was another method for self-discovery, exactly what I was working on for myself. But engaging in activities in relationship with others was a whole new experience for me.

I realized that I really enjoyed the classroom activities. At the end of each group activity, we would debrief. We were asked to engage in introspection by sharing what thoughts, feelings, and behaviors came up during the activity. It became obvious that the way we responded or reacted during these activities was really the way we think, feel, and act in real life. It created a consciousness, which is the first step to making any change.

For our last class, we met on a Saturday at a challenge course at Philhaven Hospital in Lebanon, Pennsylvania. I just assumed we would be doing some more group activities outside. And we did, but it was not what I expected...

Competition No More

Saturday came and I was quite anxious. New group problem-solving activities were being introduced to us, and we would be tackling them in the woods. However, the difference was that these activities were to take place on platforms, wooden structures, logs, cables, and other props. I loved the fact that we were outside in nature.

Fun, challenging activities were presented to the group and at the conclusion of each activity, we shared our feelings, thoughts, and behaviors.

The group bonded more than ever, and trust was earned as we supported each other during several of these team-building activities. Debriefs led to us becoming conscious of our negative self-talk and fears. We discussed our strengths and the significant roles we played while engaging in the activities. Equally important was becoming aware of *how* we were relating to each other.

One of the activities required the group to split into two. All of us, except for one member of each group, were given a stepping stone, a 12-inch-square piece of Styrofoam® covered with duct tape. Our challenge was to cross a 40-foot grassy area without falling off the stones. There were other restrictions in the group activity that required us to physically help each other. If any one person was to fall off, the whole group had to start over.

For some reason, my group *volunteered* me to be the leader. Because my objective every day was to face my fears, I accepted. We briefly talked about strategies to succeed in this activity and then we got started.

As I led the group across the field, I noticed that the other group was starting to catch up. It was clear that if we did not move faster, the other group was going to get to the finish line first. But, happily, we got there first and a burst of cheers came out of the mouths of my comrades.

Our facilitator, Dennis, started to debrief. "So," he asked, "what happened?" Members of my group started to exclaim, "We won!" Dennis looked at the group and said, "Did I tell you that this was a competition? How did I frontload this activity?" As we reflected, we realized that he had merely said that the objective was to get your group over the finish line. He said nothing about competing with the other group.

At that point I realized that my mindset has always been about competition. Society has groomed all of us to be competitive. And with a competitive swimming background, it was ingrained in me. As soon as I saw another team engaged in this activity, my mind went into the competition mode. And for what? Did that mindset help anyone? We would have been successful even if we had crossed the finish line after the other group. And, for that matter, each group could have collaborated by offering suggestions for each other.

This activity changed my life. I started to realize how most people in our society define success by winning. In *The 22 (Non-Negotiable) Laws of Wellness,* author Greg Anderson describes his "Law of Win/Win" within the context of four paradigms of social interaction. He notes that a win-loss scenario always has a loser. In the sports world, that is acceptable, providing it is done for fun and in a sportsmanlike manner. But in order to have a win-win scenario, it requires people to compromise, collaborate, and do what's in the best interests of everyone.[xv] It saddens me to this day to see how many people are still competing to win and then feel worthless when they don't.

Taking Fears to a New Height

Lunch time came and we were all very enthused, not realizing what was next on the itinerary. After we finished eating, the instructor took us back out into a different section of the forest. There were no longer any props on the ground. Instead, I looked up and saw cables 30 feet high, as well as trees for climbing, zip lines for flying, and platforms for diving.

Harnesses were given out with instructions by our facilitators, and we were gently introduced to the high elements. It was hard enough facing my fears on the ground. Now this was literally taking my fears to a new height!

Everyone was to choose his/her *challenge of choice* and set a goal that would take us out of our comfort zones. For me, the thought of climbing a tree 30 feet off the ground was already frightening. Even though I was in a harness and was to be belayed by the instructor, my mind was racing with a lot of fear.

When it was my turn to climb, my heart was pounding. Every step I took required me to focus in the present moment. If I were to look down or let my mind wander, I probably would not have gone farther. When there were no more staples on the tree, I was to step out onto a wire cable and walk across it while holding on to two other cables. My knees were shaking uncontrollably as I stepped onto the cable. The rest of the class was below, shouting words of encouragement. I proceeded to take one step at a time. The wire was extremely wobbly and it took all the strength I could muster to get to the tree on the other side. When I touched the tree, there were cries of victory from below. Everyone was so excited that I had succeeded. Free falling backwards to come back to the ground was actually fun.

When my feet hit the ground, I was met with hugs and congratulations by several other classmates. It made me aware of how essential it is to have support and encouragement to meet our goals. There was no way in hell that I would have done this on my own.

During the debrief, we analyzed our feelings that came up during the activity. I realized that I was successful with this activity due to the support I was given, but I wondered what it would have been like had I failed.

There Is No Such Thing as Failure

I had enjoyed taking this course so much that I decided to enroll in classes that would enable me to be a challenge course facilitator. This was a huge step for me as there appeared to be some technical things that I had to learn. And technology and I are like oil and water.

One of the first things we had to learn to do was to tie knots. I was able to tie various knots successfully after several attempts but soon found out that I would forget how to do it if I did not practice it daily. Besides knot tying, we learned how to belay, or attach a secure rope around a person for safety. Setting up the belay was confusing, but I found the actual belaying of another person to be easy.

As I started to do more of these new things, I found myself very aware of my thoughts. When an emotion came up, I followed it to my thought. It often turned out to be an issue where my thoughts were around *I can't do this*. Feeling incapable of doing something created a lot of frustration. Understanding that our thoughts create our reality, I realized that the more I thought it, the more it happened.

I decided to share my feelings with the class and the instructor, and by doing so, I released some of these fears. No longer did I feel I had to be perfect. Everyone understood that technology and mechanics are two of my weakest areas. So I was given the extra support and guidance that I required.

One afternoon, we were taken to a new high element on the course. I was excited to try it as I had become more confident with my other successes. I still recognized that I had some trust issues, though, as I would request Dennis to belay me instead of my classmates.

Upon walking across the cable that was 30 feet off the ground, I got to a spot where I was to reach for a diagonal cable that was literally eight feet away from me. This would require me to let go of everything and trust. I stood there, paralyzed, for quite a while. In my mind, there was no way I was going to reach it. I didn't know what to do.

If I tell the instructor I can't do it and request to come down, I fail. If I try to reach it and fall, I also fail. I didn't want to fail, so I just stood there...frozen. I don't know how long I stood there. It felt like an hour but it was probably only about five minutes. Words of encouragement came from the class, and finally I went for it. To this day, I have no idea how I was able to grab the line, but I did. I realized that I had to go for it and take the chance of failing. I also realized that to fall was so scary, even though I was being belayed.

A fellow classmate, Andrew, started climbing the tree that led to the activity on the cable that I had just completed. He walked out to the point where I froze, stood there for a moment, grabbed his belay rope, and fell backwards to the ground yelling, "There is no such thing as failure!"

What does he mean, "There is no such thing as failure"? We processed this activity afterwards and Andy explained his definition of failure. It was an "aha" moment for me. I listened to those words and for the first time understood what he meant. I had an epiphany.

All my life I had been thinking that I had to know everything and be perfect. I thought that I had to be perfect to be loved. My parents and teachers would reward me every time I did something well and punish me if I made a mistake or did poorly. So failure was not an option...*up until now.*

This was a turning point in my life where these experiential activities showed me that I had to let go of the need to know what lies ahead. It was a time to release some of the old tapes about perfectionism. It was a time to recognize that the only failure in life is not trying. It was a time to know that life is more about paying attention to the journey and less about the outcome. It was a time to give myself a break. And I was so glad I did.

Forgiveness

Probably one of the most important things I had to do to attain inner peace in my life was to resolve conflict with myself and others. As I looked back onto my life, I thought of the people who had hurt me in one way or another. I realized that as long as I held onto any anger, bitterness, or regrets, they would energetically create blocks for my evolution. I knew that if I were to release these negative emotions, I would receive the clarity I needed to move forward in my life.

I took time to review my past with many of the people in my life and determine if I had any unresolved issues with them by consciously replaying the memory. I would enter a meditative state and visualize myself telling the person how I felt about the hurtful event. I would allow myself to feel any emotion that would come up. When I was done talking, I let the other person tell his/her story. Their version of the story was often different than mine. To listen to their interpretation of the event was eye opening. Sometimes I would get an apology. But I was not there to argue; I was there to just listen and respect the other person's feelings. Often this experience led to reconciliation. It was very freeing.

I made it a point to become conscious of any uncomfortable thoughts and feelings that would arise daily as I related to different people in my life. When this happened, I looked at the people from my past who might have evoked similar feelings with their words or actions. I felt that the people in my present-day life were showing up and providing opportunities for me to release unresolved, stuffed emotions. It was important for me to acknowledge these emotions, surrender to them, and let them pass through me. Holding on to emotions was no longer an option.

Relationships are mirrors. I believe that what I see in others is really a part of myself being reflected back to me. I believe that I am all that I see. So when I see positive qualities in a person that I aspire to having, I have to recognize that I have those, too! But when I am quick to judge someone and label them with a negative characteristic, I need to remember that it is part of me as well.

According to Debbie Ford, author of *The Dark Side of the Light Chasers,* these shadow parts of ourselves are our sub-personalities that we see as unacceptable. If we do not embrace the dark side of ourselves, we are out of touch with our total being. These parts actually do offer us gifts if we choose to listen to their voice of wisdom. xvi

I remember taking Debbie Ford's workshop at Omega Institute in New York. She had us engage in one activity where we were asked to identify some behavior that triggered an angry emotion in each of us. I thought of a neighbor who had recently been very inconsiderate and did things even after we politely asked her not to. Debbie then had us take turns standing in front of three people from class and exclaim that we were that behavior. In my circumstance, it required me to say, "I am inconsiderate."

I stood there and looked into the eyes of my group in an effort to claim that part of me. I recited the phrase many times until I started to cry. What I had come to realize was that I was denying that part of me. Obviously, there were times in my life that I was inconsiderate. But instead of being willing to see it as part of my shadow, I would judge others. By claiming this as part of myself, I was coming into wholeness. And, mysteriously, my neighbor never displayed any more inconsiderate behaviors.

I believe that forgiveness isn't about condoning other people's behaviors; it frees you up and takes you off the hook. As long as your energy is holding on to old memories and accompanying emotions of anger and bitterness, you will not be able to grow. In order to discover your true essence and potential, you must release the things that no longer serve you.

Creating your own ritual in nature can be a great way to help you let go of stuck emotions. Using the elements in nature as a metaphor can be a powerful tool for releasing. You can use fire for burning, water for flushing, air for floating, or earth for burying to release the emotions and energy of the person who needs to be forgiven. It can be very powerful and freeing.

In my situations, once I was able to forgive, I realized that the people who had hurt me were doing the best they could at the time. And as I looked more deeply into each experience, I found that these painful events were actually opportunities in disguise. They connected me with a deeper part of my soul and I was able to grow stronger, both personally and spiritually.

Looking back, I am able to see the gift in every experience and every relationship. I have no regrets.

*"Because God is never cruel, there is a reason for all things.
We must know the pain of loss; because if we never knew
it, we would have no compassion for others, and we would
become monsters of self-regard, creatures of unalloyed self-
interest. The terrible pain of loss teaches humility to our
prideful kind, has the power to soften uncaring hearts, to
make a better person of a good one."*

– Dean Koontz, *The Darkest Evening of the Year*

When I thought about my upbringing, I realized that my
parents did the best they knew how based on their
upbringing. Neither of them had parents who displayed
affection for their children. Their learned behaviors were
passed down to me. By releasing pent up emotions and
forgiving them, I was able to create a new, beautiful, and
loving relationship with them.

With my personal and spiritual growth and the desire to
create a life with meaning, I was able to start expressing
my love to my parents. I finally broke the chain of
unexpressed affection one day as my father was going into
open heart surgery. I told him, "I love you." I could feel
his heart swell. He said, "I love you, too." His heart had
opened in more ways than one. Ever since then, any
conversation with my father has ended with us expressing
our love for each other.

Learning to forgive one's self is equally important. The
last thing we need to do is carry around guilt, an emotion
that is crippling. We have to recognize that we are only
human and sometimes we make mistakes. We need to let
go of the past by saying we are sorry to the parties
involved; but if we are unable to do that for whatever

reason, sharing our feelings with a trusted source can help us release our self-imprisonment.

Activities

My parents loved each other and demonstrated that to the end. However, back then it was typical for the woman to stay home, take care of the house, and raise the kids. Everything revolved around the man of the house. It was not the way I wanted to live. Our society was changing and I wanted to enter the professional world. However, both of my marriages to men emulated the traditional marriage in some way. I often felt like a maid while still holding a full-time job.

Once I became conscious of what a healthy relationship looked like, I was determined to be in one. However, I knew I had to heal before I was ready for another relationship. The following are questions and exercises that I practiced to help me understand my codependency so I could relate better to others. Hopefully, they will lead to you having respectful, loving relationships with others as well.

1. Describe the relationship between your parents. How have your relationships with significant others been similar?

2. Identify the healthy and unhealthy characteristics in your relationships with others using the following checklist. Which characteristics do you offer in a relationship? What characteristics have been displayed by your partner(s)?

Healthy Relationships include:

- Expression of love and affection, verbally and physically
- Trust
- Support
- Encouragement of the other to become their best self
- Honesty
- Openness
- Appropriate expression of feelings
- Separate friends
- Separate interests

Unhealthy Relationships include:

- Fear, neediness, and insecurities
- Control and manipulation
- Lack of trust
- Jealousy
- Inability to communicate on a deep level
- Dishonesty
- Enmeshment
- Only having the same friends

- Giving up your interests
- Lack of affection
- Being emotionally unavailable
- Abuse: physical, mental, emotional, verbal, or sexual

3. Think of an uncomfortable situation that requires you to communicate your feelings to someone. Write down an "I message" that you can use to express your feelings appropriately. Start with "I," name your emotion, and then state the behavior of the person that made you feel that way and the result of the behavior.

    Example: "I am so angry when you promise to let the dog out and you don't, and now she's had an accident on the new rug." (Remember to stop and say nothing else after this.)

4. It's important to have a trusted friend and a support system. What is something you have wanted to do but have procrastinated doing because of your fear of failure? Write down how you would feel if you never tried it. What's the first baby step that you can take to move toward your goal? Who can support you on this?

5. Name three people with their positive qualities that you aspire to having:

   a.

   b.

   c.

   Do not look ahead until you complete the above.

After completing this activity, know that you have these qualities or you wouldn't be able to see them in others. "All that I see, I am."

Now name three people with their negative characteristics that you dislike immensely.

a.

b.

c.

These characteristics are your shadows. Claim them as part of yourself.

6. Who are the people toward whom you still hold anger, bitterness, or regret? What about? Communicate your feelings to them using appropriate, yet assertive, communication.

If you are unable to communicate this to them because they are deceased, violent, or in a position to make your circumstances unbearable, find a way to release the emotion. Designate an object to "be" that person. Pace, scream, and say what needs to be said from your gut. Ask the Universe to help you "feel" if you often operate from your head instead of your heart.

7. Forgiving yourself is vitally important. Identify the things that you have done that still evoke shame or guilt. Create a ritual in which you write them down, make amends, burn the list, and release these things to the Universe saying, "I'm sorry. Please forgive me." Apologize to the affected parties by talking or writing to them, if possible.

Chapter 6: From Pain to Purpose

It has been over 20 years since my spiritual awakening. A day does not go by where I am not conscious of my thoughts, feelings, and actions. When challenges arise, I look at them as opportunities for growth rather than problems to be solved. I strive to be the best version of myself and know that I will continue to do that until I take my last breath.

My story demonstrates that my painful experience served as a catalyst for me to discover a pathway to peace, power, passion, and, eventually, my purpose. Choosing to consciously develop loving relationships with myself, others, and the Universe was essential for me to heal and live authentically. The more I resolved conflict with myself and others, the more clarity I received in understanding my true essence and potential. Upon discovering my gifts and my purpose, I no longer ask the question about the meaning of life...

> *"Your purpose in life is to find your purpose and give your whole heart and soul to it."*
> – Gautama Buddha

Gratitude

The gratitude that I have for all of my past lessons is overwhelming. I have gone from a lonely life to an extraordinary life. I have shifted my thoughts from *out there* to *in here*. I have moved out of the victim role into that of a leader.

When I review my life and realize how much it has transformed, it blows me away. The things I thought I would never be capable of doing are exactly the things I am doing. I never thought this journey of self-discovery would lead me to finding out that I am more than I thought I was. By facing my fears and releasing the things that did not benefit my growth, I was able to find my gifts that were hidden from me but were always there.

There are no mistakes in life. Yes, I have veered off of my sacred path at times, but the Universe has then provided opportunities to get me right back where I belong. Sometimes these opportunities were challenging because I had to face the shadow parts of myself and feel my emotions. However, by having a strong relationship with *Spirit*, I knew I was going to be protected. In retrospect, I am grateful for those challenges as they connected me with the deepest parts of my soul and reminded me who I am and who I am not.

Attracting a New Kind of Love

As I continued to work on myself after my relationship crisis, I found I became more and more empowered. I tried new things and faced my fears on a daily basis. I became educated on the characteristics of healthy and unhealthy relationships. I understood the difference between the things that I am capable of controlling in my life and the things that I have no control over. And when things happened that were not necessarily the way I had hoped for, I knew there was a reason for it.

As I healed from my divorce and relationship with my ex-lover, I took time to look at what I had been attracting in my life and why. I was able to understand connections with the kind of men that I invited into my life. In one way or another, the men of my past shared similar characteristics with those of my father. The Universe had presented these relationships to me as opportunities, repeating past issues that needed to be resolved. It was no longer about me pointing the finger and judging. It was about me learning to step into a strong sense of Self, becoming self-reliant, and relating to others in a new way.

The energy of striving to feel loved was a continuation of my childhood needs. The Universe continued to give me the lessons I needed to learn by presenting people in my life who were emotionally distant or controlling. Once I learned the lesson that you can only receive the amount of love based on how much you love yourself, my *Higher Power* offered me a new relationship with a new lesson.

Four years after my divorce, I felt ready to start dating again. I made an extensive list of what I was looking for in a relationship. Shortly thereafter, I met a man who seemed to fit the bill because he was kind and had many qualities on the list. I was not sure I wanted to get married again; but after dating me for three years, he proposed and I accepted. We married the following year.

This marriage was different than both my first marriage and my relationship with my ex-lover. This relationship offered me independence and the ability to communicate appropriately, but it lacked passion. It left me feeling less than desirable and, at times, unlovable. It also felt one-sided, with me juggling a full-time job with the majority of household responsibilities. I fell back into the role of "Donna Reed."

In hindsight, I believe I subconsciously chose this man out of fear of getting too close to someone again. I believe I was trying to avoid another passionate, addictive relationship like I experienced with my ex-lover. I did not want to experience that kind of hurt again. I thought that this new relationship was what true love was supposed to feel like...calm and safe.

I loved this man but was not "in love" with him. My heart was not totally invested in it. That became obvious six years later when I met someone at work who stole my heart. I was not looking for another relationship. What started out as a friendship turned into a strong attraction.

Once again, the Universe presented me with a challenge that forced me to look at my truth. When I started to feel sensations in my heart space for my co-worker, I was confused. I asked the Universe for clarity, and events transpired where I got my answers. In my heart of hearts, I knew this relationship would offer me a fulfillment like I never had before.

The biggest challenge was that I had fallen in love with a woman! Was I a lesbian? Did I ever think about having sex with a woman before? Looking back, I remember having a crush on a girl from my swim team when I was 13. But I didn't know about sex at that time. Plus, with my strict upbringing, it hadn't even become a thought. I had to do a lot of introspection.

What I discovered was that when you love someone, male or female, the physical affection just happens. I believe that as we evolve into a higher consciousness and become less egoic, we fall in love with a soul. We don't see gender.

It was important for me to remain open and honest with my husband. After I told him that I had feelings for a woman and wanted to explore the relationship, he and I separated. We continued to communicate and I expressed my heartfelt sorrow. He did not understand it and was devastated. But I was at a point in my life where I had done so much work on myself that I knew my truth. It was the end of my old identity as a heterosexual. A few months later, I asked for a divorce and established a beautiful relationship with the person I consider my soul mate, Diane.

There is absolutely no way that I would have entered a relationship with a woman without healing from codependency. My concerns about other people's opinions would have prohibited me from taking the leap. My mission of remaining true to myself had become the most important thing for me to do.

I finally feel I have entered the healthiest relationship of my life. Diane and I not only share an intense love for each other but we both feel comfortable in disclosing our feelings. Our communication is honest and expressed in appropriate ways. We are free to be who we are while striving to be the best versions of ourselves. We support and encourage each other to fulfill each other's dreams.

We have an equal, committed partnership with a lot of trust. We admire each other's qualities and laugh together at our imperfections. Our relationship is one of interdependence; we can function independently but then come together intimately, without neediness and insecurities.

As I look back over my relationship history, I absolutely have no regrets about any of my chosen partners. There were lessons to be had in all my relationships. As much as I may have felt hurt or unloved, I, too, am sorry for hurting my partners with my codependent behaviors. Each relationship offered a gift to everyone. It is my hope that my ex-partners found the gifts of our relationships and used them as stepping stones to enter healthier partnerships where more lessons were to be learned.

New Abilities

As I continued to become conscious of my thoughts, feelings, and actions, I was able to get clear on my intentions for doing things. It became important for me to be authentic and not do things for the wrong reason. No longer did I allow my ego to lead the way with fear-based thoughts. Needing recognition, valuing other's opinions more than my own, comparing myself to others, feeling desperate for love, giving a lot more than receiving, feeling less than, and needing to be liked were some of the codependent patterns that I was able to release. Of course, I can still feel these attitudes sneak in at times, but I now have tools to keep them at bay.

After having released so many blocked emotions, I started to recognize my true essence and potential. I began to remember who I am and why I am here. As I continued to let go of trying to control everything in my life and let the Universe lead the way, I found myself becoming more intuitive.

The connection with *Spirit* had become very strong. I was able to hear my inner voice more clearly as I no longer had a lot of *noise* from other voices of the past in my head. I was operating from a place of love within my heart space and less from my fear-based ego. Having experienced so many hurtful events in my life, both as the receiver and the giver, I had learned my lessons that spoke the message, "Who am I to judge?" I was given the gift of compassion.

I started to do Sacred Path Card readings for my friends and had amazing feedback. The card readings helped many people, both men and women, transform their lives by giving them direction. I realized that I had become a channel and was being told by *Spirit* what I should say to each person. The cards provided a great tool for self-discovery with lessons that each individual needed to learn.

Walking My Talk

As I continued to do introspection, I was being told by *Spirit* to use my gifts to help heal and empower others. My resistance to starting a business was great, but I still felt compelled to start one. My new life was amazing and my passion to share my success story with others was overwhelming. But some of my codependent limiting beliefs started to surface.

I was still teaching in the high school and had several years before retiring. I thought if I started a part-time business now, I could do what I loved when I retired. But my limiting thoughts were *Who am I to start a business? I don't know the first thing to do.* As much as I felt confident in empowering others, my fear about having a business kept me from starting one.

Finally, I realized that if I wanted to help empower other women, I had to walk my talk. I had to face my fears and remember the importance of asking for help when needed. It is hard to do things alone. So I asked the Universe for guidance. And, once again, the Universe answered...

A new opportunity arose at my high school for me to become the wellness consultant for a "school within the school." It was organized by a science teacher and was created for students who were interested in Environmental Science. The theme was also based on Native American teachings and traditions! It sounded interesting and I needed change. But in order to serve on this faculty, I would be required to create a Wellness Curriculum for the students.

Although I was not trained to write a curriculum, I chose to face my fears and step into this new role. I decided to include some of the mind, body, and spiritual tools that helped me transform as part of my plan. I felt strongly that the students needed to engage in self-discovery and strengthen their relationships with themselves and others. The activities that I would incorporate would allow the students to get in touch with not only the physical aspect of wellness but the mental, emotional, and spiritual aspects as well.

The curriculum included my facilitation of health classes, experiential learning activities for self-discovery, and physical fitness programs. I also networked with others to create sub-contracted programs such as white water rafting, horseback riding, scuba diving, and Native American teachings.

Finding the right people to help me with the program was very synchronistic. Learning that Native American teachings were part of the overall curriculum, I contacted Shadow Wolf. She was excited to become part of the program and agreed to teach Native lessons to the students.

The students loved Shadow Wolf. She engaged them in various fire ceremonies with incredible stories that led to critical thinking and self-discovery. She presented the stories in a way that each listener would determine what the lesson of the story was to him/her. She also had the students create tools of empowerment with mask making, personal shields, and medicine bags. She relayed messages in nature from animals and explained how the world is our mirror.

We all learned a lot from her. What I came to realize upon experiencing her rituals and ceremonies in nature was that I had been doing similar things! I found that my self-taught shamanic practices were really Spirit-led and my teachers were starting to show up to help me hone my skills. The overall wellness curriculum was very successful, and I started to realize that *I am* capable of creating something unique with my newfound abilities.

As I re-visited the idea of becoming a life coach and creating a business, the words "there is no such thing as failure" continued to play out in my mind. My thought was that the only regret I might ever have would be not trying.

My business would be based on my knowledge as a Health/Aquatics/Physical Education teacher combined with the wisdom and tools I had acquired due to my own transformation. Based on my experience, I felt I could best help women in transition who were interested in personal and spiritual growth. My business would incorporate the three components that I learned were essential for my healing and total transformation: deepening loving connections with self, others, and the Universe.

When I looked at my gifts of organizing and intuition, coupled with my wisdom, I decided that retreats would offer the best experience for the women. Travel is transformational in itself! What better way to slow down and connect with your true essence and potential! Not only are you away from the busy pace of everyday living but you are nurtured in a loving and supportive atmosphere that allows your heart to open to your authentic self. And, most importantly, I felt that retreats would be perfect and allow me to create experiential activities for each of the three essential components for healing!

The only question that remained was, "Where should I run my first retreat?" While I was still married to my second husband, an opportunity arose where I was offered free air miles to go anywhere in the United States. For some reason, Hawaii popped into my mind. I had never been there before and felt a pull to check it out.

Assuming my then-husband would not want to join me, I felt the Big Island would be a safe place to visit by myself. As I investigated places to stay, I came across an eco-spa, B & B called "The Dragonfly Ranch." It was near the ancient Place of Refuge, a healing sanctuary, as well as Honaunau Bay, which was great for snorkeling. I knew this was where I wanted to stay.

Upon trying to make flight arrangements, I ran into a problem. There were many blackout dates. The only week available was the week of our anniversary. I was correct in assuming that my husband did not want to go. He insisted that I should still make the reservation, but I felt badly and did not know what to do. So the next morning I put the question out to the Universe...

That afternoon, I decided to go swimming at a friend's house. Prior to her joining me, I got on a raft in her pool and looked up at the sky. Within moments, dragonflies started to fly above me, just inches from my face. Was that a sign? Are the dragonflies leading me to the "Dragonfly Ranch" in Hawaii? I took it as a sign but was still feeling confused. Perhaps I was reading into it.

Later that day, I made plans to have dinner with a friend at a new restaurant. She told me that she would meet me at the outside bar and save me a seat. When I arrived, I noticed that all of the barstools were occupied except for the one next to her. Upon sitting down, I looked in front of me and noticed a large, hanging dragonfly candle. It was the only dragonfly candle at the bar. I gasped, and my friend asked me if I was okay. I responded by telling her that the dragonfly was perhaps a sign that I needed to go to Hawaii.

She said, "Oh, just wait..."

Seconds later, the bar maid approached me to take my order. She was wearing a huge dragonfly necklace. I turned to my friend and said, "Guess what? I'm going to Hawaii!"

I made the reservations and a few weeks later I was on my way to the Big Island. As soon as I stepped off the plane, I could feel the concentrated spiritual energy of Hawaii and how powerful my connection was to all of creation. I was already sensing that I was going to experience one of the most mystical and magical places on earth.

As I experienced the island, I became aware of the numerous synchronicities that were occurring. Serendipitously, I met Dr. Susan Gregg, an author and former apprentice of Don Miguel Ruiz. Her book entitled *Finding Your Sacred Self* was one of the first books that highly resonated with me upon my spiritual awakening in the 90's. Susan not only performed an energy session for me in the hot ponds but also agreed to be a guest facilitator if I chose to run my retreats in Hawaii.

This trip was transformative for me. It was obvious that "dragonfly medicine" was primarily responsible for my shift. Dragonflies had appeared everywhere I went. I had learned that the spiritual meaning of a dragonfly totem is for one to gain a new perspective and make a change. I knew it was time for me to step into my true essence and potential. I was being called to see through the illusions and let my light shine.

Hawaii, the Island of Healing, offered everything that I envisioned for a retreat. The destruction and creation of this volcanic island show us that we, too, can experience devastation and rebuild our lives to become more beautiful than we could ever imagine.

With a newfound confidence and a decision to follow through on my vision, I completed my life coaching certification program and registered my new business, *Phoenix Adventures in Wellness,* in 2005. I liked the name *Phoenix* because it represented the mythical bird rising from the ashes. It was symbolic of my death and rebirth that occurred as a result of my relationship crises. Later that year, I facilitated my first successful retreat to the magical, mystical Big Island of Hawaii!

Living My Purpose

Who would have thought that I would be running retreats in exotic destinations? I used to be a woman who was afraid of her own shadow and was now leading retreats to help empower other women! Not only do I help other women discover their true essence and potential but I do it in places that are highly energetic and magical. Finding perfect retreat venues in Hawaii, Peru, Utah, California, Pennsylvania, and New Jersey were synchronistic experiences and ended up being ideal for enabling transformation.

It became obvious to me that *Spirit* was in charge because there was no way that I, alone, could have created some of the mystical experiences that occurred on the retreats: different people showing up when we needed them for answers and then disappearing as if they were never there; dreams and cards predicting that something would be occurring later that day and it actually happened; and fish magically encircling us while snorkeling to wish us farewell. These are things that can only happen in partnership with *Spirit*. These were examples of mystical things that happened, congruent with our intentions that were set on the first day of the retreat.

To further describe the power of intentions, I wrote a blog after a mystical experience on a Hawaii retreat in 2012:

The world is our mirror. When I run a retreat, I make my clients aware that the outer world reflects what is happening in their inner world. I tell them to become conscious of their environment, especially the behaviors of animals, insects, birds, and reptiles.

On the first full day of my "Whales, Women, and Wisdom" retreat in Hawaii, I took four powerful women on a whale watching excursion. I briefed them about whale behaviors and told them to pay attention to the symbolism. If the whales were blowing, they were telling us to release what no longer serves us. If they were diving, we were to go to the depths of our souls and feel our emotions. But hopefully we would also see them breaching, jumping high out of the water, which was about coming into our true selves!

The experience was incredible, with whales appearing in every direction. With all five of us on the bow, we were able to witness a constant display of the whales blowing, slapping, and diving. The experience was exhilarating as we laughed and vocalized requests for more of the same!

The waves started to kick up more than usual that day, blessing us with an occasional spray of ocean water on our warm bodies. The only thing left to see was a full breaching of the whales. So we continued our shouting to "bring it on!"

All of a sudden, a giant wave engulfed the right side of the bow and immediately filled the bow with three feet of water. The pummeling of this wave took me down and had me under water in the bow within a nanosecond. Under normal circumstances, the bilge pump would have drained the water instantly. But at that moment, the pump failed and the bow of the boat started to sink rapidly.

Our boat captain shouted, "Everyone to the stern! Now!" Three of the women from the retreat immediately moved to the stern while I was being helped by another woman in our group to get to my feet. Being the only one who was banged and bruised, I sloshed through the water to find myself falling again as my leg became temporarily trapped under a bench with bins floating around me. Watching people's possessions float off into the ocean, I was the last one to get to the back of the boat.

Finally, in the stern, we helped each other don inflatable snorkeling vests. (The life vests were in a hatch under three feet of water so we were unable to use them.) We stood there in awe as we watched our boat captain maneuver the boat, call for help, and give instructions to his first mate and others during this emergency. Everyone felt emotionally paralyzed, wondering if our boat was going to sink before we were rescued. Several minutes later, another whale watching boat came to our rescue.

As our captain helped his 20 passengers jump from the railing of our boat into the arms of the captain of the other boat, I noticed some movement around the two vessels. Less than a hundred yards away, five whales surrounded the boats and they were breaching.

After safely jumping to the other boat, we were taken back to shore and found out later that our captain was able to save his boat. We processed this event for the rest of the retreat, uncovering why the Universe had given us this experience. Knowing that there is a gift in every experience, we realized that we had set intentions to discover more of our true selves, "go with the flow," and create deeper connections with each other. This near death experience certainly did all of that. It will go down as one of the most memorable, enlightening experiences of our lives.

There is always a gift from every experience. To label the gifts as good or bad doesn't matter. They just are. Asking ourselves "why?" and finding the gift will allow us to see life in a whole new way.

Encountering some of these magical experiences was a catalyst for altering many of the women's ways of seeing things. Often, the women went home feeling like they were a part of everything and everything was a part of them. Although some of the women were going home to empty houses as they were grieving relationships that had ended through death or divorce, they had experienced a connection like never before that would enable them to never feel alone again.

Since 2005, I had continued to expand *Phoenix Adventures in Wellness* with more workshops, retreats, card readings, and individual coaching sessions. As my business grew, both with successes and struggles, I grew. Having a business allowed me to get in touch with more of my limiting beliefs. It became a perfect opportunity to face more fears and master my relationship skills.

As I received testimonials from clients about how I had become a catalyst in their transformation, it was very humbling. One of my favorite experiences was with a client who came to me for a card reading because a friend of his "paid it forward." He sent this testimonial:

"I sat out back tonight wondering how I got here. Two months ago I was given a session with Kathleen by a friend. I went to my session with an open mind and an open heart. I needed a change, both in job and in my personal life. Both were going nowhere. Immediately after my reading, which was powerful and motivating, I went on a journey that led me to an amazing new job, and I'm living in a beautiful house on a golf course in Washington state, a place I've wanted to come back to for years.

How did I know this was my path? I found every one of the cards from my session along the way. Each one showed itself to me at the time I needed to see it. The opportunities in life keep coming back to me every day. In a whirlwind of six weeks I have been transformed – gave up nearly all of my possessions, both physical and emotional, and I now experience the calm presence that I was looking for in my life.

I have so much gratitude for Kathleen and for my friend who paid it forward to me, and the line of friends who paid it forward before her. What was started by someone long ago has turned into an amazing storyline of transformation in many lives. Take the time to be present, sit with Kathleen, and discover how to take back your life!"
– Will K., Vancouver, Washington

What was interesting about Will's reading was that one of the cards he pulled was the "Shawl" card. I told him it was about "returning home." Often this card means that one needs to let go of fear-based ego and return home to the place of the loving heart. [xvii] I told Will, however, it can mean different things to each person.

Will sat there for a moment, just staring at this card. It had a picture of a waterfall on a heart-shaped mountain. He told me it reminded him of Washington. And then he told me about the opportunity he had for a job interview in the state of Washington, almost 3,000 miles away. He had been considering returning there someday.

Will decided to take the interview and almost immediately got offered the job. While in Washington, as mentioned in his testimonial, he consciously looked for messages as guidance about whether or not to take it.

One day he went hiking and got the sign that needed no explanation. He sent me a picture of a waterfall on a heart-shaped mountain. It was identical to the picture on the Sacred Path card! It was confirmation that this was exactly the place where he needed to be. He moved and has never been happier.

Receiving feedback from others was heartwarming and validating. I was doing what I loved, but I still felt that there was something missing.

Where Am I Now?

After retiring from 34 years of teaching high school in Pennsylvania, I had a feeling that I wanted to move out of state but I didn't know where. I also knew that my wife, Diane, had to get to a point where she could feel comfortable moving her business as a financial educator to another state.

I often thought that California or Hawaii would be the next place of residence. My brother and father lived in California and I loved the weather. But in January of 2015, I became a grandmother. My son, daughter-in-law, and grandson live in Pennsylvania. My other son lives in New York. Moving west was not an option. I was back to square one.

In April of 2015, my close friend, Dianna, asked me to help her find a house in Rehoboth Beach, Delaware. She had formerly lived in the Lehigh Valley of Pennsylvania, rented a home in Rehoboth to heal from a broken marriage, and now was choosing to stay there and buy a house.

I was excited to help Dianna so I drove to Rehoboth Beach and we began the house hunting. Upon searching for homes for her on the computer, I came across an active adult community that looked amazing. It was located in the town of Lewes, which is on the Delaware Bay and borders Rehoboth Beach. The website described the development as being on a two-mile lake with a kayak launch and abounding with nature. It was comprised of new single story homes offering open floor plans and a clubhouse with a beautiful outdoor swimming pool. Although it was not what she was interested in, I asked Dianna if we could go look at it the following day. Being the sweet soul that she is, she not only agreed but was excited at the thought that I would consider moving there.

The next day I looked at the model homes and explored the community and fell in love with it. I called my wife, Diane, who came down that weekend to see it for herself. She asked me, "Can you live here?" I responded, "I think I can!" Without hesitation, we made a decision to go home, sell our house, and move to Lewes.

Talk about a strong feeling! Who makes those kinds of decisions without looking at other homes in other places? Mysteriously, we have heard the same thing from other people who have spontaneously moved into this area.

The move out of Pennsylvania was trying for me. I had lived in the Lehigh Valley all of my life. It was hard to leave our renovated 1850's farmhouse on our magical, beautiful one-acre property. But I made a conscious decision to release it and move to a location that was calling to me. I didn't know why, but Lewes, Delaware, was where I needed to be.

Upon moving here, I learned that we are living in the region of the Cape Henlopen Triangle, an area where there have been strange paranormal occurrences for over 300 years. Freakish mirages, storms in perfect weather, UFO sightings, showers of falling stars, and mystical sea creatures were just some of the stories that still plague scientists and are unexplainable to this day. [xviii] Who knows why so many people are feeling pulled to move here? For me, it sounds intriguing and I feel it will be a perfect venue for future retreats. It has great magical energy and will be transformational for many.

During the year of our move, I traveled to California a few times to work with an internationally famous shamanic practitioner, Dr. Steven Farmer. I felt compelled to claim my gifts and knew that he could help me hone my skills in shamanism. I was attracted to study with Dr. Farmer as he and I shared the same philosophies and mission. Upon reading his book *Earth Magic*, I discovered that we spoke the same language when it came to healing. After becoming certified as an Earth Magic® Practitioner, I incorporated ancient healing methods in my practice to help clients restore connections to their souls. The program was powerful as it took me to the next level of my soul's evolution.

Incorporating shamanic treatments into my business has been the missing piece. It is a practice that focuses on the spiritual cause of an illness, whether it is physical, mental, or emotional. Unresolved traumatic experiences can lead to the dissociation of parts of one's soul. This fragmentation is the soul's way of protecting itself. This soul loss can make one feel depressed, empty, alienated, obsessive, or out of control. Sensing that something is missing is another sign that a *soul retrieval* needs to be performed. [xix] This treatment is ideal for recovering codependents as many codependents state that they feel like lost souls.

Although I had engaged in personal shamanic journeying for many years, my codependent insecurities and limiting beliefs had kept me from being able to claim my gifts. A few months after moving to Lewes, I dissolved my Pennsylvania business of *Phoenix Adventures in Wellness, LLC*. Releasing it was another challenging, soulful experience, but I knew it was an opportunity to start anew. After settling into our new home, I registered my new shamanic coaching business, *Heart Rock Healing*. I chose the name to indicate that my practice is powerful and yet full of love.

Recently, I performed a *soul retrieval* for a client. Shortly thereafter, I received this testimonial from her:

"I've been trying to place this feeling I have had for the past two days, trying to make sense of it. It's like pure joy running through my veins. Kathy told me it may take up to three days for me to feel the change. Oh, I feel it. I'm a writer, but putting this into words feels beyond me. I have to try.

I spent my life standing in the shadow of other people's fear, anger, and beliefs. This is the first time I have felt the essence of pure joy, pure love without attachment. It's the first time I've felt the essence of me. It was there when I was young, hiding from the fear, anger, and judgment of my family. It played around with coming out when I was in my 20's. The day I got married, this part of me sadly packed her bags and left, knowing she could not exist in the depths of my husband's anger and hostility.

She's back. And it's sometimes overwhelming, but it's a good overwhelming. I feel like my home base is coming from a place of vulnerability and love without attachment, like it's my norm now instead of a place I strive for and sometimes reach.

I planted a seed once that yielded a crop beyond my wildest dreams. I did it from a place of love and vulnerability to help a friend. I could have never imagined the beautiful love story it would grow into. My love story. I realize that when I consciously plant seeds from this place of love and vulnerability, the universe is working with me, and synchronicities happen that can't be put into words or explained. These are the seeds I want to plant, consciously, with intent, not just for me, but for the world.

I missed the essence of me. Thanks for bringing her back."
– Tina S., Richmond, VA

Embracing the intangible by trusting *Spirit* and my guides has demonstrated that there is so much more to life than we realize. Shamanism has been around for thousands of years and is still being practiced because of its ability to mend the soul. To deny that there is anything more than what meets the eye is unreasonable.

Creating Conscious Communities

Besides offering individual healing sessions, my soul has nudged me to take it to the next level, where I can have a larger impact. Creating healthy and conscious communities has become another one of my main goals. There is no time to play it small anymore. It is a critical period and we need to do what we can to bring about peace and harmony in our society. We need to unite as one big human family, recognizing that we have more in common than we thought.

Unity in a community starts with the transformation of individuals moving from their heads, where fear and ego reside, and into their hearts, where only love resides. I am doing what I can to help others shift their consciousness and recognize that they are love, loved, and lovable, with unique gifts to offer the world. My message is to create an understanding that unity is always possible providing that all parties are open to appropriate communication. Teaching the keys to creating and sustaining healthy, conscious communities will be through speaking engagements, seminars, and workshops.

As a retired teacher, I am reaching out to schools as they can be significant in making this change happen. Schools are the best source for teaching social skills, a reverence for all of creation, and overall wellness because of their ability to reach everybody. Incorporating this type of curriculum needs to become a priority. Our world needs to learn how to get along and respect each other's differences.

Facilitating fun, team-building activities with large groups in the schools is one of my passions. The students enjoy them tremendously and the results are transformative. The experiential learning activities give students an opportunity to engage in critical thinking and understand who they are. Respecting others and communicating appropriately are social skills that have been lost and are essential to learn in today's times.

If you'd like to get more information and learn about an opportunity for transformation in your own school, group, or organization, go to my website at http://kathleenmcginley.net/services/heartrock-healing.

Life Talks

As a woman who has gone from feeling invisible to invincible, I have come to believe that any woman is capable of stepping into her power if she chooses. My personal success story was the catalyst for starting my business. My "mess" became my message.

One of my workshops that has helped empower women is called "Life Talks." This is a wise women's circle that allows positive, like-minded women to come together for support and love while on their sacred paths. Using the Sacred Path Cards for pre-selected monthly topics, I encourage everyone to share their deepest feelings and thoughts on the teaching. A talking stick is provided for the woman who is doing the speaking. There is no cross talk or judgment; it is a safe place for all to be who they are. For many women, this is the first time that they feel heard and respected. It is a great opportunity for women to learn to use their voice as well as feel part of a community that supports a vision of peace, love, and joy for the world.

HUGS for Harmony

One of my newest programs, HUGS for Harmony, is a four-part, year-long series for women who are interested in transforming their lives through self-healing, deepening their connection to spirit, and discovering their purpose. It has components of:

H--Healing

U--Universal Oneness

G--Gifts

S--Service

HUGS programs are designed for various groups with special interests and are offered at different times of the year. For example, one HUGS program is for women in recovery from unhealthy or codependent relationships. It offers healing, support, and a new outlook on life. With the release of a relationship that no longer serves a woman may come a feeling that there is a reason for her trials and tribulations. It is customized for the woman who feels that this challenge is a *soul call* prompting her to discover who she *really* is and who she came here to be.

Through healing and empowering activities, group support, and a willingness to become the best version of herself, this program allows each woman to see how her challenges are opportunities that can awaken her soul, thus leading her to her true self. Creating a more meaningful life and finding her purpose require her to heal her past and connect with her truth as she deepens relationships with herself and the Universe. By doing this, she will release fear, live in love, discover her gifts, and receive clarity on how she can serve the world to make it a better place.

H--Healing: Part One of this program emphasizes healing the past, re-gaining identities, increasing self-esteem, and managing stress so that each woman can move forward in her life again.

U--Universal Oneness: Once the loving connection with self is deepened, Part Two emphasizes creating harmony with others and recognizing that we are one with the Universe.

G--Gifts: Part Three involves supporting each other to find one's passions, strengths, gifts, and purpose.

S--Service: Finally, Part Four provides support for each woman as she steps into empowered action and leadership, using her gifts to help make a difference in the world.

Thus, the HUGS program is for women who are willing to undergo transformation through extensive healing, who are interested in furthering their personal and spiritual growth and redefining their role in society, and who are ready to step into their power.

Participants will meet in the area of the beautiful beach town of Rehoboth Beach, Delaware, for four long weekends during the year. With enough interest, there may be other opportunities to conduct HUGS programs in other areas of the country. On-line group support and periodic group video calling will take place in between the in-person sessions.

If you'd like more information about HUGS, go to http://www.kathleenmcginley.net.

Conclusion

I love my life...all of it! My journey has been an incredible ride with a story about how I broke many patterns of codependency using practical and mystical strategies. Having had the courage to answer my *soul call* has led me to developing the most loving relationships I have ever had and living a life I never thought possible.

I believe our mission here on planet Earth is to remember who we are and who we came here to be. But becoming authentic and discovering your soul's purpose requires you to know and love every part of your Self. It requires you to recognize that we are all one. It requires you to embrace the intangible...

And by doing so, you will live the magical and fulfilled life you were meant to live!

> *"We cannot be ourselves, unless we know ourselves."*
> – Thomas Merton, *No Man Is an Island*

Notes

[i] Dr. Steven Farmer, *Earth Magic* (Hay House, Inc. 2013), 208-209.

[ii] Melodie Beattie, *Codependent No More* (Hazelden Foundation, 1992), 34.

[iii] Beattie, 39-52.

[iv] Co-Dependents' Anonymous International, *"What Happened?"* Web www.coda.org (May 2016).

[v] Coda.org, *"The Twelve Steps of Co-Dependents Anonymous"* (May 2016).

[vi] Coda.org, *"The Twelve Steps of Co-Dependents Anonymous"* (May 2016).

[vii] Coda.org, *"The Twelve Traditions of Co-Dependents Anonymous"* (May 2016).

[viii] Jamie Sams, *Sacred Path Cards: The Discovery of Self through Native Teachings* (HarperSanFrancisco, 1990), 273-277.

[ix] Andrews, Ted, *Animal-Speak* (Llewellyn Publications, 1996), 1-6.

[x] White Bear, Helen, Lou, *Dreamspeak* (See of Tranquility, 1977), 103.

[xi] American Heart Association, *"Is Broken Heart Syndrome Real?"* Web http://www.heart.org/HEARTORG/Conditions/More/ Cardiomyopathy/Is-Broken-Heart-Syndrome- Real_UCM_448547_Article.jsp#.V0hL4fkrLIU (April 18, 2016).

[xii] David Gershon and Gail Straub, *Empowerment: The Art of Creating Your Life as You Want* (Dell Publishing, 1989), 25.

[xiii] Susan Gregg, *Finding Your Sacred Self* (Llewellyn Publications, 1997), 23.

[xiv] Gershon and Straub, 30.

[xv] Greg Anderson, *The 22 (Non-Negotiable) Laws of Wellness* (HarperSanFrancisco, 1995), 103-110.

[xvi] Debbie Ford, *The Dark Side of the Light Chasers* (Berkley Publishing Group, 1998), 99.

[xvii] Sams, 261-265.

[xviii] George Contant, "Inside the Henlopen Triangle," *Delaware Beach Life*, Holiday 2015, 62.

[xix] Dr. Steven Farmer, 209-210.

About the Author

Kathleen McGinley is a loving mother, grandmother, and wife who has spent her life helping people become better versions of themselves. As a high school teacher in Pennsylvania for 34 years, she touched many of her students' lives by teaching them how to utilize some of the skills mentioned in *Soul Lost, Soul Restored: A Sacred Journey Back to Self* to create successful, meaningful lives.

In 2005, Kathleen started her own business, *Phoenix Adventures in Wellness*, with a mission to empower and teach individuals the skills to navigate the trials and tribulations of today's world. Since moving to Delaware in 2015, she has continued her vision with her new business, *Heart Rock Healing*, employing new initiatives in an attempt to unite the world.

Kathleen expanded her business after studying with Dr. Steven Farmer, an internationally recognized shamanic practitioner and psychotherapist. She now incorporates her intuitive and spiritual healing practice to help individuals restore balance of mind, body, and spirit. Kathleen is passionate when engaging people in experiences in self-discovery as she helps them come into alignment with their truths so they can create meaningful lives they never thought possible!

Made in the USA
Coppell, TX
27 October 2020

40343195R00066